BRICK
BUY BRICK

LEASE OPTIONS

Matador
9 Priory Business Park,
Wistow Road, Kibworth Beauchamp,
Leicestershire. LE8 0RX
Tel: (+44) 116 279 2299
Fax: (+44) 116 279 2277
Email: books@troubador.co.uk
Web: www.troubador.co.uk/matador

ISBN 978 1783064 397

British Library Cataloguing in Publication Data.
A catalogue record for this book is available from the British Library.

Typeset by Troubador Publishing Ltd, Leicester, UK
Printed and bound in the UK by TJ International, Padstow, Cornwall

Matador is an imprint of Troubador Publishing Ltd

MIX
Paper from
responsible sources
FSC® C013056

INTRODUCTION

This book in the Brick Buy Brick educational series has been written in association with Tigrent Learning UK, the UK's most respected provider of professional training programmes.

Tigrent and its associated network of industry experts and partners have a wealth of property investing knowledge. Tigrent trainers and customers derive from all ages and backgrounds and have over a decade's experience of working with new and existing investors from all over the world.

This book in the Brick Buy Brick series looks at Lease Options as an investment strategy and the opportunities it offers to the property investor. It examines the ins and outs of Lease Options, which

includes Purchase Options, Sale Options and Sandwich Options, plus the topic of Rent To Buy. It explains the USPs of Lease Options, and explains how to find the right opportunities which make a profit.

For more information and to give us any feedback on your reading experience, please visit:

www.brick-buy-brick.co.uk.

CHAPTER ONE

WHY LEASE OPTIONS?

How would you like to buy a property for a pound?

That's what Lease Options can give you the power to do. It is one of the lowest cost ways of adding a property to your portfolio.

A Lease Option is a type of contract that allows you to lease or rent a property from someone for a set period of time with the option, but not the obligation, to purchase at the end of the term. It gives you what Donald Trump calls 'control' – which in many ways is more powerful than ownership.

Types of Lease Options?

Lease Options is an umbrella title covering:

Purchase Options (where you are buying property from a vendor) & Sale Options (where you are selling your property to a buyer).

A Lease gives you the right to rent out the property. An Option gives you the right, but not the obligation, to buy.

A Purchase Option is often short-term and grants the holder the freedom to buy the property at an agreed price within a specified period of time.

A Lease Option is a Purchase Option with the added freedom for the holder to lease or use the property during the Option period.

Put simply, Options are written agreements that give the holder choice or freedom. Depending on the wording in the document, the owner gives exclusive

2

freedom to buy, use or sell the property, or a combination of these freedoms. If the buyer chooses to buy whilst the Option is in place, the seller must sell. That is the essence of an Option.

Why Lease Options?

Lease Options are causing quite a buzz in the investment market and people increasingly want to know about them. Investors are interested in Lease Options for these key reasons:

Lease Options allow you to generate a monthly income from a property that you don't own.

Lease Options give you the benefit of the capital growth of the property.

Lease Options are a good investment strategy because they don't require huge financial resources.

Background to Lease Options

Lease Options are well established in the commercial market, where a business will often lease a property and have an option to purchase, but they have not

3

been traditionally used in the residential market.

Roadblocks to traditional property buying

Why would someone choose to look at a Lease Option over the traditional ways of buying property?

Bank Qualifying

Traditional property buying often means having to find a big deposit, having to qualify for a bank loan and needing a good credit score. These are all things you don't need when it comes to Lease Options.

Landlording

Becoming a landlord traditionally means devoting a lot of time to managing and looking after a property. Many who get into building a property portfolio find themselves saddled with a full-time job they don't really want which involves all the hassle of maintaining a property. Not with Lease Options.

4

Refurbishing

The cost of having to refurbish a distressed property can be prohibitive. Lease Options can be a solution to the home owner and take the responsibility for a poorly maintained property out of their hands.

Regulations

At the moment, Lease Options are not yet regulated, but it makes sense to behave as if regulation does exist, because it may come in at some point and you will want to be prepared. In essence this means behaving in a way that is fair and reasonable. One good practice is to draw up a Heads of Terms – a single page setting out what you and the seller are agreeing to do before you approach a solicitor to draw up official contracts (see Chapter 8).

Options are created by circumstances. Either someone has a distressed property or someone is a distressed owner (someone dealing with a marriage

break-up, with financial problems, a need to leave the country, etc.).

What you've got to look out for is: How much money a vender needs now. Do they need all the equity from a property straight away? In some circumstances they might not. They might be down-sizing, the property might be one received in a will, or a host of other reasons. Seeking out the reasons for a sale will be the key to finding the opportunity for a Lease Option (see Chapter 4).

CHAPTER TWO

PURCHASE OPTIONS

Let's look at Purchase Options in more detail.

You find a property worth £120K
The outstanding mortgage is £110K

When you speak to the vendor, they agree to a Purchase Option. This means that they agree to you paying or 'babysitting' their mortgage for them.

You have 4 things to consider.

1. The price of the property

You will want to offer a good price for the property

and normally this will be close to the market value. But rather than agree to give the vendor this money now, you might say that you will give them this price in five years' time. This period of time is called 'the term'.

2. Upfront payment

This is the money that you agree you will pay now and this amount is flexible. In many cases this may only need to be a token payment to enact the Purchase Option, for example £1. Remember that this is actually the smallest amount possible to offer. Perhaps the most famous recent case of property being exchanged for such a sum occurred in 2005 when the Labour government sold the Millennium Dome for the nominal sum of £1 to Meridian Delta, the consortium behind Bluewater shopping centre in Kent. The amount of the upfront payment depends on *what the vendor needs*. In many cases the vendor just wants the burden of the property and its mortgage payments taken off their hands, especially if the property is proving difficult to sell or

they are in financial difficulties. In some cases this upfront payment might need to cover the cost of the vendor's legal fees, or it might need to cover the cost of the vendor re-locating to a different area. When you speak to the vendor it is important to find out not what they want, but what they need and the upfront payment should reflect this.

3. The monthly payment

This is the amount that you will pay per month to cover the vendor's mortgage. It needs to be low in relation to the rental price that the property can garner.

4. The Term

This is the period of time the Option will run. It might run less than or as long as the remaining term on the mortgage but it cannot run longer than the remaining term on the mortgage.

Overall, it is important to have at least two exit

strategies. The property must work on a buy-to-let basis in its existing state in case you cannot increase the value by adding more rooms. Depending on the property you need to ask yourself the following questions:

Can you:
Set up an Option and sell?
Refurbish the property and sell?
Put a tenant into the property and hold?
Rent out the rooms for higher cash-flow?
Convert into flats and sell them separately?
(This last question will depend on demand – what kind of properties are in demand in the area? In some areas there is a higher need for small flats, for example in university towns or near hospitals).

The more yes's you have to these questions, the greater the opportunity for a Purchase Option.

The Advantages of Purchase Options

It takes the banks out of the equation.
Credit scores are unimportant.

Monthly payments are negotiable.

There is a huge lender fee saving.

There is very little cash involved.

It is control of a property without ownership.

The pathway to profit

Investors who are looking for Purchase Options are looking to solve problems. The determining factor of vendors agreeing to a Purchase Option could be the relief of financial problems. The property could also for some reason be a problem to the vendor. The benefits to the seller of a Purchase Option might be breathing space from these financial problems and the chance to get on with their life. Investors seeking Lease Options are essentially looking for problems, but the good news is that these problems can make profit for you.

CHAPTER THREE

SALE OPTIONS & RENT TO BUY

A Sale Option is an Option on a property you already own or control.

For the purposes of Lease Options a Sale Option means Rent To Buy. Putting together a Sale Option means you are offering someone the chance to rent the property now and the opportunity to purchase it in the future, in other words to Rent To Buy.

Rent To Buy

Rent To Buy is a simple Lease Option strategy that works well in all kinds of markets. It tends to attract

responsible tenants with the mentality of home-owners, who want to stay in a property a long time and treat the place like a home rather than just a house.

Rent To Buy is attractive to people looking for property because it allows them to rent the property now and buy it later – when they are ready to. It gives someone the flexibility to choose the best rate of finance at the best time and also allows them to avoid the large fees and deposit normally required for a traditional purchase.

Identifying a property for Rent To Buy

A good Rent To Buy property needs to be in a good area or one that is up and coming. In other words an *aspirational* area. To identify an aspirational area you will need look at the types of property, the shops and the general feel of the area. Ask yourself 'Is this somewhere young professionals will want to live?'

The Tenant Buyer

A Tenant Buyer is different from a straightforward tenant in a crucial way. Under the terms of the Lease Option agreement the Tenant Buyer undertakes to do any work on the property themselves. This means that any value they add to the property will benefit them because in doing so the value of the property that they agree to eventually buy increases. This also means that if the boiler breaks down the Tenant Buyer is responsible for its repair. If they refuse to replace the boiler themselves, this will invalidate their option to buy, the Lease Option falls away and they become a straightforward tenant.

Identifying a Tenant Buyer

What makes a good Tenant Buyer? You will need to ask yourself: Do they have a good job? Do they have good money making ability? Do they already have money saved for a new home?' Ideally, you will want them to have all three of these things.

It's not difficult to make Rent To Buy an attractive proposition to someone. The key question is 'how would you like to secure your ideal home without having to go to the bank first?' Understandably many people are all ears at this point!

Becoming a Tenant Buyer gives someone the opportunity to literally 'try before they buy'. It also allows them to build equity in a property while they rent. It's easy to illustrate the advantages over renting to someone. Rather than their rent going into a black hole it goes towards actually buying their property. Plus, any improvements the Tenant Buyer makes to their property adds value to the property from day one.

Finding Tenant Buyers

How can you find potential Tenant Buyers? One strategy is to ask mortgage brokers if they can refer people to you. There will be some people who go to mortgage brokers because they wish to purchase a property in a conventional way and find they cannot get a mortgage. As long as the reason is due to

15

something like too low an income for example, then they could be a potential Tenant Buyer.

Letting Agents could also be a good place to go to find Tenant Buyers. Again, you need to work out what the aspirational areas are and visit lettings agents in those areas. They may well be able to direct you towards people who wish to Rent To Buy.

It is important to remember that in order to do a Sale Option (Rent To Buy) you should actually have control of a property first – unless you want to be an estate agent!

Advertising is another key way to find Tenant Buyers, on websites like Gumtree or by using so-called 'goldmine ads' (See Chapter 5).

Tenant Buyer Questionnaire

When you are trying to find a suitable Tenant Buyer for your property it is well worth finding out the following:

What they already know about Rent To Buy. Do they understand what it is?

Where they currently live.

Whether they currently own or rent. If they already own a house, why are they wanting to buy another? It is important to understand their current position and what they're trying to achieve. They could own a flat but want to up-size, in which case you should ask why they haven't tried to get a mortgage. There might be good reasons for this, especially if they've just moved here from overseas and haven't been in the country long in which case they are good potential Tenant Buyers.

What they currently pay in rent or mortgage.

What area they want to live in.

How many bedrooms they want.

How many people will be living with them.

How much can they afford to pay as a monthly payment towards the purchase of their new home (Naturally what they can afford is exactly what you need!)

How much deposit have they saved? Their answer will be, again, exactly what you need!

How soon were they looking to move into their new home.

If the property needs work, it can be a very good idea to find a Tenant Buyer with the skills to do it up, like a builder, a plumber or electrician.

A typical Sale Option scenario

You have a property valued at £130,000.

You offer the Tenant Buyer the chance to purchase the property at £130,000 over the next five years.

You set out that the Tenant Buyer's monthly rental payment will be £600.

In addition to the monthly rental payment the Tenant Buyer will also pay a rental top-up payment of £150 per month. This is a contribution towards the Tenant Buyer's deposit when they decide to exercise the option to buy at the end of the five year term.

You will require a payment from the Tenant Buyer to get into the deal. It's a very good idea at this point to ask how much a potential Tenant Buyer already has saved for their house. If they say £40,000 then you can answer 'that's exactly what I need!' This upfront amount is flexible, however, and 3% of the purchase price would be considered fair and reasonable.

3% of the purchase price in this scenario, where the property was £130,000, would be £3,900.

It is always important to remember the flexibility of

all Lease Options. If the Tenant Buyer can afford to pay you more than a rental top up of £150, then you might want to increase this amount.

Once the Tenant Buyer reaches the end of the 5 year term, this is what they will have paid to you in addition to the monthly payment:

Upfront cash: £3,900
Top-up payment £150 per month for 5 years (60 months): £9,000
TOTAL: £12,900

The Tenant Buyer will then go to a mortgage broker. You have already agreed the purchase price of £130,000, so if they find a 90% loan to value mortgage, they will need to find 10% for the deposit, which is £13,000. As we can see above, they have already paid £12,900 towards the deposit, so they only have a remaining £100 to find.

When you are collecting the monthly payments it is strongly advisable to keep the monthly payment and

the top-up payment separate and put the £150 p/m into one account and the £600 p/m in another to make sure you don't spend your Tenant Buyer's deposit money.

Your goal is that when you come to the end of the term, they have basically paid their deposit in full. Using this as a rule of thumb will work out the length of the term and how much they pay per month.

Your protection from risk

For a Rent To Buy you will need two documents: a Lease Option Agreement and a normal Buy To Let Tenancy Agreement.

As soon as there is non payment of rent or rental top-up, the agreement falls away and the protection for you is the tenancy agreement. All the upfront money is non-refundable. Therefore if the Option is not exercised, you are not hurt. You can go through standard eviction procedures to remove the tenant.

An Option agreement is very flexible. On both a Purchase Option and Sale Option you can agree what you want between all parties before you set up a contract with two sets of solicitors. You can state the terms you wish; for example that the Option term is extendable after 5 years if the Tenant Buyer decides they can't yet buy after 5 years. You can state in writing that the tradespeople the Tenant Buyer employs need to be reputable and so on.

In the scenario above the Tenant Buyer has the option but not the obligation to buy the property at any time within the five year term.

In terms of responsibility for buildings insurance in a Sale Option, you should obtain a building insurance agreement with both your name and the Tenant Buyer's name on it but it's advisable that you should pay for buildings insurance because it will give you protection. In the same way, you should also pay for your annual gas safety checks because this will protect you and your investment in the long run.

Pros of Sale Options for investors

It's a hands-free investment – you don't have to constantly visit the property like a landlord.

The Tenant Buyer is responsible for maintenance and repair.

You don't need to employ the services of a property management company.

Pros of Sale Options for Tenant Buyers

They need as little as 3% of the property purchase price to 'get in' to the deal.

They can add value to the property and they themselves gain from the increase in value because they've already agreed to pay a fixed sum for the property.

Past credit history is not a hindrance.

It's an easier way to get onto the property ladder.

It's a way of building equity in a property while renting.

Sandwich Options

One form of Lease Option is a Sandwich Option which involves both a Sale Option and a Purchase Option *with the same property*.

You might have done a deal with a vendor (a Purchase Option) and rather than you being the end buyer, you have decided to pass the property onto a Tenant Buyer.

You are basically sitting in the middle of a Purchase Option and a Sale Option on the same property and managing the relationship between the vendor and the buyer.

Advantages of a Sandwich Option

The cashflow you make from a Sandwich Option is the difference between what you've agreed with the vendor for babysitting their mortgage and what you are getting from the Tenant Buyer. You could, for instance, be paying £300 p/m on the Purchase Option but receiving £600 p/m from the Tenant Buyer.

In basic terms the advantage of this strategy is that it allows you to create money-making opportunities at every stage of the deal; up front, in the middle and at the back end when you sell the property at an increased price from that agreed with the vendor.

CHAPTER FOUR

THE SELLER'S MOTIVATION

Why would someone want to agree to a
Purchase Option?

In order to find Purchase Option opportunities it is essential to understand the motivations behind someone agreeing to such a deal. It is also important to be familiar with the possible objections, fears and prejudices that a vendor may have about a Purchase Option in order to set their mind at rest and point out the benefits to them.

The reluctant seller

There are a number of reasons why sellers can be reluctant. They might find themselves in negative equity or they might have higher sale price expectations than the actual value of the property, for example.

There are a number of strategies that you can employ with a reluctant seller but the key is to talk to them, learn about their situation and understand their circumstances. This will help you understand their motivation to sell and may open up the opportunity for a Purchase Option.

In order to maximise your profits you will normally be looking to purchase a property at below market value. The way you can express this to a vendor is that you are looking to buy properties *wholesale* in order to put them back on the market.

Naturally vendors are going to be reluctant to sell at less than the market price but you need to dig deep

27

and find out the reasons for the sale. There are reasons that mean some people will need to move quickly. They might need to leave the country because a visa has expired, they may need to leave the area for personal reasons, because of harassment, for instance.

An example of a Below Market Value
(BMV) purchase.

In this case you will be utilising a Purchase Option to purchase the property.

Property market value: £100,000 – £110,000
Refurbishment costs: £0 – £8,000
(If you decide to rent at the low end, you won't necessarily need to do anything to the property but you could decide to improve the property to attract a better rental price)
Deposit @ 25% = £23,750

Revaluation (based on new kitchen or bathroom): £120,000

In this scenario above your maximum BMV offer might be: £80,000

The vendor says they will accept no less than: £95,000

Breaking the stalemate:

In this situation where the vendor wants £95,000 and our offer is a maximum of £80,000 we could do the following:

We can agree to the price of £95,000 but say we will pay in three years.

Price agreed: £95,000.

Length of Term: 3 years

Upfront Payment @ 4.21% of £95,000: £4,000

So you would give the vendor £4,000 up front now, you would take over the vendor's mortgage payments and you would pay the vendor the remaining £91,000 in three years' time.

So in this case you just need £4K to do a Purchase Option. You then have control over the property and can rent it out.

N.B. You will need to get consent from the bank for permission to let before you can rent out the property. In most cases this is simply a formality.

In all Purchase Option cases it is important that when you agree to cover the vendor's mortgage that you are not paying the mortgage money directly to the vendor. You need to protect yourself against the possibility that the vendor does not pay their mortgage, meaning the house could be repossessed. Regardless of the risk of losing your investment, imagine how traumatic repossession notices would be to your new tenants in the property! This is why it is important to set up a special bank account in the seller's name into which you pay the monthly mortgage amount and from where the mortgage payments go to the bank, thus absolving the seller from making the payments themselves.

Why would someone agree to a Purchase Option?

It is important to understand the reasons why people might want to take a Purchase Option. You are looking for owners *needing* to sell rather than merely *wanting* to sell and there might be a number of reasons for this. They may have lost their job or got into debt, the owner may have died and the executors of the will might want to get rid of the house quickly. The property might have problem tenants and it has become a burden to the seller. The seller might be leaving the country, downsizing, moving to a different area, experiencing ill health, or getting divorced.

There are countless reasons why a seller might need to sell quickly and this is why you will need to start a conversation, albeit tactfully and sensitively, and build a relationship with a seller in order to discover their motivation to sell. Doing so will help you identify the opportunities for a Purchase Option.

CHAPTER FIVE

MARKETING

The key to marketing your property business is to identify your potential customers, so who exactly might your customers be? Who are those that might be looking to enter into a Purchase Option?

Tired or reluctant landlords

They are generally running the property business on their own, they have a number of properties spread over the country and it's become a bit of a job that they can't or don't want to handle.

Retiring landlords

They have now taken on the tenant's responsibilities. They don't always need to sell as soon as possible because the properties have a small or no mortgage.

Pension investor

They never wanted to be a landlord in the first place, they just wanted a pension from a property. These are often older couples who bought a house in order to sell it for a profit. However, all they wanted was this profit rather than having to manage the property, deal with the legal side of being an investor, deal with tenants, and so on.

Accidental landlords

These are people who upsized when the market was low and wanted to rent the property for a few years only, but have found themselves renting out their properties while they wait for the market to improve.

33

Inheritance landlords

Those who have inherited a property. In these cases there might be a lot of people involved, for example four people might be named on the will as beneficiaries.

The fringe investor

They have often bought their property through an investment club and have little understanding of the property market. They are cash-rich, time-poor people who have no rental experience, might have a number of properties dotted over the country and are experiencing high vacancies in a tough climate.

Private sellers

Those who want, for whatever reason, to by-pass the estate agent.

Divorce cases

Where both parties cannot reach an agreement on how to split the property.

Negative equity cases

When there is no capital in the property. In these cases it is important to write the Option at a price which settles the finance on the property.

What NOT to look for

Beware of strange, quirky or unusual properties like lighthouses, windmills, etc. Just because you can get a Purchase Option on a church, it's not always a good idea to do it. You must always think about a property's rental potential.

Beware saturated markets. Be careful that you don't buy in an area where there isn't enough existing demand for what is already there.

Finding sellers

There are three main things to remember with marketing your property business and finding motivated sellers:

You need at least 5-7 marketing strategies for your business.

You need to be talking directly to sellers (rather than going through estate agents).

You need to get your phone ringing.

Harnessing the power of estate agents

The local estate agent can be a very powerful ally in your property investment career, if you know how to get the best out of him. Your credibility as a property investor is key so it's worthwhile having a pack of relevant documents which show you're serious, including a 'hunting brief' of the kinds of properties you're looking for and (particularly useful if you're searching for properties in negative equity) a 'proof of funds' letter – verification from a financial

institution of the availability of funds to complete transactions. The most important thing to do when it comes to estate agents, however, is to build a relationship with them, which takes some time, but the first thing you can do is make sure you are talking to the right person.

Know your estate agent

In a typical high street estate agent you tend to find the same kinds of characters and by learning to identify them you can speed up your progress and get the most out of them.

'The Tweeter'. This is the school leaver. In his downtime you'll mainly find him on Twitter. He's just started and not usually very knowledgeable.

'The Market Trader'. He's in his early twenties and hungry to do deals. He'll ring you often but his property knowledge isn't that great.

'The Saturday Noser'. This person does the Saturday

viewings only. Their job is just to drive clients to look round empty properties on a Saturday. They're likely to be key-holders who have no knowledge about the vendors and might not even work in the office.

'The Twin-Set & Pearls'. This may be a man or a woman but typically an older woman who has been in the property industry for a long time, has seen it all and is incredibly efficient.

The 'Twin Set & Pearls' is someone you want to cultivate a professional relationship with because their insider knowledge can be invaluable to you. They are the sort who will alert you to a property chain breaking down, and who'll remember to ring you when a problem property or problem vendor crosses their path.

'The Alan Sugar'. The independent estate agent. This character owns an independent estate agent so they are more entrepreneurial and play by their own rules. From them you'll get a lot more knowledge of landlords wanting to move from letting to selling.

They are normally the sole decision maker so they don't have to pass things up to the regional manager, for instance, and slow things down.

Your estate agent strategy

When you walk into an estate agent's office for the first time your immediate priority is to find the decision maker, which may not be the first person who greets you as you walk through the door. You may well find yourself sitting down with the Tweeter! You might ask if there is someone in the office who deals with property investors, which in turn may attract the attention of the all-important Twin Set & Pearls.

It is important to set out straight away what you are looking for in terms of area, as well as your price band. It is crucial to speak to the decision maker as soon as possible. One way to speed up this process is to ask the kind of questions that only the decision maker would be in a position to answer like 'How much work does a particular property need?', 'What do you think the expected value will be after

39

refurbishment?', 'what's the reason for the sale?' These are the kinds of enquiries that depend on in-depth knowledge and asking them not only marks you out as a serious investor but also helps you get to the senior estate agent more quickly.

When discussing a property you should try and get the clearest possible picture of both the property and the seller to see if it fits the criteria for a Lease Option. You might want to ask how long the property has been on the market or whether it's been put on the market previously with another estate agent. If either is the case then this suggests that the property is having difficulty selling which might alert you to the possibility of a Lease Option.

Some investors might be uncomfortable with suggesting a Lease Option over a traditional purchase, so it's important to give thought to how you get Lease Options 'onto the table'. If you've used Lease Options before then setting out an instance where you 'helped someone else' is a good way in. Portraying Lease Options as a possible solution to a

difficult situation – which it is – is a helpful way of introducing it as a way to go. In any case, however, building up a relationship of trust with an estate agent is crucial before you start talking about any kind of creative deal. This relationship won't happen immediately, it is to be cultivated over time, by visiting an estate agent regularly, perhaps once a month, finding out which properties aren't selling and what the problem properties are.

Letting Agents

Letting agents can also help a property investor looking for Lease Option opportunities. You should be looking for independent letting agents and, especially, motivated landlords who have high vacancy rates and are struggling to let. The key, again, is to talk to people, find the relevant person who deals with lettings only, and build a rapport. You are trying to identify landlords who might be looking to sell portfolios and it could be well worth offering a finder's fee to the lettings agent if they can help you find these opportunities.

Gold Mine Adverts

These are simply advertisements that you place in newspapers and relevant websites which are designed to attract potential sellers. Here is an example of a good gold mine ad:

Company director looking to buy a 3 bed + house for long term lease with a view to purchase. Call Sarah 0161 XXX XXXX

You'll notice the ad mentions a woman's name. In the psychology of advertising it has been found that people are more inclined to call a woman than a man. Don't let this discourage you if you are a male property investor, you can still use a woman's name and when your phone rings say that you are Sarah's colleague and you can help. Remember, you just want to get the phone ringing.

Use a telephone number that's local to the area. A local number is more appealing than a mobile number, and less expensive to the caller. It also

suggests a stronger local link with the area which makes it more inviting. There are companies from whom you can rent a local telephone number diverted to your mobile phone.

Other advertisement examples:

Professional tenant looking for 5 year lease. Call Sarah 0161 XXX XXXX

Local investor will pay £10K more for your property. Call Sarah 0161 XXX XXXX

In the above example you will indeed pay this figure but you will do so in ten years – this strategy will get you calls and then you can negotiate from there.

Before you hand the keys to the bank call Sarah 0161 XXX XXXX

The above example is a good way of attracting people who want to avoid repossession.

Successful Gold Mine advertising

Look at the design style of the papers you are advertising in and try to stand out. It pays dividends to be different from other ads in terms of background colour, size, etc.

A weekly paper is better than a daily paper to advertise in and works out to be more economical.

Check the readership of different papers and go for one with the highest readership (a simple phone call to the paper will give you this).

Check that the details on your advertisement are correct, especially the phone number.

Remember, the longer you want your ad to run for, the cheaper it will be.

Ask for a voucher copy (a free copy of the ad) to be sent or emailed to you. This will allow you to check your ad before publication and will help you if you

are investing in an area that is far from where you are based.

If your ad is aimed at people with financial problems it makes sense to place it in the free local paper rather than in a paid-for paper.

Leaflets

Leaflets can be DIY or professional.

They are very area dependent and work better in some areas than others. With all your marketing strategies you will need to experiment, see which ones are most effective and refine to use those that give the best results.

DIY leaflets

DIY leaflets are an excellent marketing tool. They are cheap to make, and it is their very 'home-made' quality which makes them more attractive than a professionally printed leaflet.

DIY leaflets should be handwritten in big black marker and make it clear that you are looking for a single property. It should say something like this:

I'm looking to buy a home in your area. I am willing to pay market price for the right property. I am not in a chain and can move quickly.

The campaign: It is important to send out your leaflet for at least eight weeks. Marketing psychology tells us that it will be binned for the first 4 or 5 times, but eventually someone might save it for a time when they do need you and this is how you get your phone to ring.

Professional leaflets

You can get a copywriter to write your leaflet and have it professionally designed. These days it need not be expensive to have a professional leaflet produced. Websites exist where one can reverse bid for the job and give the work to the person who will do it for the lowest price.

Ugly Marketing

Sometimes the uglier your advertisement is, the more successful it can be! So-called 'ugly marketing' can be remarkably effective at cutting through the 'noise' of traditional and professional advertisements, and their bespoke, 'home-made' quality can lend a welcome degree of personality and authenticity to your adverts.

Ugly marketing can take many different forms and it's an opportunity for you to use your imagination and think outside the box. 'Bandit signs' are large boards usually positioned near busy roads where they are likely to be seen by large numbers of passing motorists. A simple 'Need to sell your house?' or 'I buy houses' written on easily-read black on yellow together with a phone number can be a very straightforward way to get your phone ringing. Be aware that though not illegal, these unlicensed boards are often frowned upon by councils, so it's best to fix your board away from residential areas where they might attract the ire of the neighbourhood!

Texting

If you build a database of landlords telephone numbers from their advertisements on websites you can use a bulk text messaging service to text them your ad.

Networking

Go to local networking events and local landlords associations meetings to see if there are landlords that have some houses that are causing them hassle. Talking to people and taking the time to hear their stories can provide you with essential leads.

Rent To Buy Marketing Strategies

With Rent To Buy the idea, as always, is to get your phone ringing. You can use all the strategies above like Ugly Marketing, newspaper ads and so on. You will want to target people struggling to get a mortgage and say how you can help. With Rent To Buy, however, professionally produced

advertisements and leaflets tend to work better because you are targeting aspirational people who are looking to get on the property ladder. If you are using websites like Gumtree to advertise, make sure you include pictures of the property as people expect to see what they are being offered and won't ring if pictures aren't included. It is also important to explain in 'baby talk' exactly what Rent To Buy is. Most people won't understand terms like Purchase Option or Lease Option but will be fully versed in concepts like 'buy now pay later' or 'try before you buy'.

CHAPTER SIX

NEGOTIATING

When you are negotiating you need to find out what the seller needs. This will then help you decide the terms with the seller. It is important to arm yourself with facts before you begin your negotiation. Research the prices of properties for sale in the area. Remember to take the estimated values with a pinch of salt as these are sometimes taken as an average of similar properties and aren't always accurate. For this reason, the sold prices of properties are far more relevant to you than the for sale prices.

Arming yourself with facts

Websites like www.hometrack.co.uk can tell you a lot about the area you are thinking of investing in, from the crime rates to the performance of local schools. It is a good idea to subscribe to property valuation sites that allow you to download a report for a specific postcode to see things like the percentage sale to asking price and the average weeks to sale. Tracking the sales in the area will tell you how fast property is selling and if it's selling well, you might well think that it's not the sort of area that's right for property investing using Lease Options. It's when properties are taking on average six months or longer to sell that means it is an area where you are more likely to find potential deals. Being able to tell a seller with authority that their property is likely to take six months to sell can prove invaluable when you are looking to reduce the asking price. The Land Registry will also help you check your facts. You can find out what the property was bought for, who the lender is and if there are any secured charges against the property.

Interacting with the seller

Most Lease Option contracts are not standard, they are uniquely created. This means you have to be clear about what you want when you talk to the vendor. It comes back to the four parameters set out in Chapter 2:

The price of the property.

The upfront payment (according to the vendor's needs).

The monthly payment (which must be low in relation to the rental) and whether it works on capital repayment. If it doesn't, can we convert the mortgage to interest only?

The length of the term (the longer the better). This can't be longer than the term of the mortgage, so if there are 18 years left on the mortgage product, the term can't go beyond that.

As a property investor you are looking to solve problems and create win-win solutions – a win for you and a win for the vendor. A good negotiating

tactic when dealing with a vendor is to ask them 'What would you like to happen?' This is a question that will help release information from the vendor, allow you to build up a fuller picture of their circumstances and help you create a deal tailored to their needs.

Understanding the vendor

It's well worth your while to use basic psychology to give yourself the advantage in negotiations. In general, people tend to sell to people they like; if someone likes you they may be more willing to accept your offer over someone else's. Therefore it can be incredibly useful to get a handle on the personality of the seller because by learning about their character you will be able to decide what negotiating approach they best respond to which will increase your negotiation success. It's not about trying to become someone you're not but it means subtly mirroring a seller's behaviour, making them feel comfortable and giving them the kind of information they need.

One tactic that helps to draw out what seller you are dealing with is to deliberately arrive five minutes late to the viewing. Different personality types can respond to this tactic in different ways:

Amiable. The amiable seller might respond to your apologies for your slight lateness with assurances that they don't mind and enquiries after your welfare, making sure nothing bad happened on your journey. The amiable type is everybody's friend, non-confrontational, emotional, attentive but often non-focused. If you offer a Lease Option to this kind of seller they will want reassurance that these kind of deals have helped people in the past and can help them, and that you will be able to 'hold their hand' throughout the process.

Socialiser. The Socialiser will bat aside your apology for lateness with a shrug, will want to talk about everything apart from the property and may prefer to do the negotiating in the pub! They are easily distracted and easily bored. Questions that you might like to ask a socialiser are 'Do you need all the

money today?' and 'if you were to sell today, what will you be doing with the cash?' These kind of enquiries will allow you to get information from a socialiser because they are focussed more on the social aspects of their life and how they would like to spend the money.

Analyser. The analyser will analyse the reasons for your lateness, like asking whether it was the roadworks on the dual carriageway. The analyser prizes being right and they respond best to facts and figures. They need to justify their decisions with facts and will need a lot of detailed information about how an Option works, whether there are contracts involved, and so on. An analyser will need the pros and cons of the Option before they make their decision.

Driver. A driver will show impatience at your lateness because they just want you in and out. Drivers are fast-paced, results driven and independent. Drivers have to know the 'win' for them in any given situation so you have to be clear and succinct about

the benefits to them of going for a Lease Option. A driver will want a decision on whether you will buy the house straight away. In which case, you should use your property report with its facts and statistics as a negotiating tool.

A negotiating system

A system for negotiating relies on the factors of:

1. Rapport
2. Pain
3. Solution

First you must build rapport with the seller and you can do this by asking questions. You might ask how long they have lived in the property, what they are going to do with the money from the property, i.e. are they looking to downsize, go into rented accommodation, live with a family member and so on. Asking a seller whether they already have another property lined up will help you determine how motivated a seller is, especially if they are

moving into rented accommodation and will shortly be faced with paying both a mortgage and rent if they can't sell now.

You need to understand if the property is causing the seller any pain because you may be in the position to alleviate that pain with a Lease Option. You might want to find out how long the property has been on the market and whether it's been on the market with any other estate agents before their current one. If the property is vacant you might want to discover the reasons for this and how much refurbishment it might need. It is helpful to you if the property does require refurbishment because part of the deal could involve you taking care of this refurbishment. Is the property in a broken chain? If so, this could also put you in a good position. Asking a seller how soon they need to complete the sale may also allow you to get a better picture of their situation. If they are very precise and give you a time limit of a specific number of weeks, this could be a clue to something about their personal situation that you may want to try and learn more about. Asking a seller what will happen

if they don't manage to sell the property is also a great question for potentially revealing the background to the need to sell and allows you to paint a picture to the seller of the consequences of the property not selling.

If the seller has no identifiable pain but is not fixated on selling quickly, they could still be up for an Option. Some sellers might be fixated on price. By saying that you can meet that price, not immediately but in five years' time, you have begun a conversation about Lease Options.

The third stage of your negotiating system is offering the seller a solution and to do this you need to understand what, in an ideal world, the seller would like to see happen. If the seller simply wants you to buy the property you might put forward a cheeky offer in a non-threatening way. You might say that while you understand and appreciate that the seller wants a certain price of around the market value you can only offer your much reduced price, however you are able to show them a way that they could get

much closer to their asking price. If the seller is interested in hearing more you could explain that just as cars can be bought using hire purchase, houses can be bought in the same way. You can explain how you can offer the seller close to their asking price, but in five years' time, and during that time you will pay their mortgage and look after the maintenance. At the end of this five year term you would buy their property at the agreed price.

Don't start off by using the words 'Lease Options' or 'Purchase Options' to the seller. Go through the benefits – the better price, take the hassle out of the sale, potentially quicker completion, getting a problem property off their back, etc.

More negotiating techniques

One way of creating breathing space to put together the right deal is to say that you have to consult with a higher authority, a business partner, before you can offer the exact terms of the deal to the seller.

If you are haggling with a seller over price, rather than splitting the difference, you could ask the seller how close they could come to your offer. This puts you in a stronger position than simply meeting half-way, after all you are offering the solution to the seller, so it should be you who are dictating the terms.

A useful technique for breaking the deadlock over price is to offer the seller what they want but extend the terms of the deal. Using this 'trade-off principle' allows you to say you will give the seller what they want but in ten years rather than five, for example.

Offering a profit share is another good option for negotiation. You can say that in addition to the purchase price you will give the seller, say 10% of any price increase after the sale. Your pitch is that they get paid when you get paid.

CHAPTER SEVEN

DUE DILIGENCE

Once you have identified a vendor who may be open to a Lease Option it is essential you carry out due diligence to protect yourself.

Before you set up a Sale Option you will need to ascertain such things as what refurbishment is required on the property and how much this will cost. You will have to work out what the property will rent for and whether there is the potential to add value via conversion to a House of Multiple Occupancy (HMO). You will also need to check that demand for the property exists in the area.

There are several parties involved in any Lease Option and the first step is to do your homework and verify you are dealing with the right person in each case. In the case of a Purchase Option you need to make sure you are doing the deal with the person with the legal title of owner. A simple check on the Land Registry will give you this information and cost you as little as £3. In the case of a probate property the homeowner is deceased, in which case the legal owner of the property will depend on the terms of the will and you need to speak to the executors of the will, as they will be in charge of who owns the house.

The mortgage

The second step for the property investor is to verify the size of the mortgage and how much of the house the lender owns. If there is no mortgage, bearing in mind our intention to be fair and reasonable in our dealings, you might factor in a payment to the owner in order to sell the deal. You will also need to check whether there are any Early Redemption Fees on the mortgage.

Remember that the mortgage term must be longer or equal to your Option term. The type of mortgage is also important; is it Residential or Buy To Let? If it is Residential, is there consent to let? An Option is still possible if there is no consent to let but it's an extra step you need to go through in order to get this permission.

You will need to confirm the size of the mortgage repayments and check what kind of mortgage it is; Capital & Repayments or Interest Only.

Are the mortgage repayment rates fixed or variable? In the case of a fixed rate mortgage, what is the rate, when does the fixed period end and what rate follows at the end of this period?

In the case of a variable rate mortgage, what is the rate and how might it change in the future?

Are there mortgage arrears? What is the amount and how many months payment does this equate to? The number of months the seller is in arrears will tell you how close they are to getting repossessed. Ask

yourself if you can afford to pay off any arrears in a lump sum up front. Can you afford for this deal to work by paying off these arrears? If you don't pay the arrears off are you risking the potential of losing the house because the bank will repossess? If the answer is yes, pay off the arrears. If paying off the arrears will still not make the Lease Option work you should find another strategy or else walk away.

Payment holidays

Is there a mortgage payment holiday in place? If so, when will it finish? Is it Interest Only now and will it later revert to Capital & Repayment? Remember, when people are out of work they may get a temporary rate from the bank. Some banks give 3-6 months on Interest Only in the event of job loss. If so, you need to find out when this period ends.

Repossession

Have letters threatening repossession been sent to the owner by the lender? If so, what stage is this at? Is a

court date set? Is there an eviction order? In all these cases the situation is salvageable and a Lease Option is still possible but time-wise things are more urgent.

Secured debt

Is there lending secured on the mortgage? If so what is the balance of the loan, the rate and the remaining term? Investors should watch out for loans taken out on the mortgage because if they are not paid the house can be repossessed. If this is the case you can split the deal so the homeowner continues to pay the loan, and you pay the mortgage.

Bankruptcy and insolvency

It is important to check that the seller isn't bankrupt. They must also have the capacity to cover payments once the Lease Option is in place. If the seller goes bankrupt during the term then the house is still their asset and could be repossessed. Thus the Lease Option agreement should be designed to put the owner back on an even keel financially.

Final checks before completion

There are further steps you may also want to complete as part of due diligence. Is the property in a flood risk area? Are there covenant restrictions on the property? Depending on the Option strategy you may need to do Local Searches but bear in mind whether they will be relevant at the end of the Purchase Option term, say in five or ten years' time, the point at which you actually purchase the property.

CHAPTER EIGHT

DEALING WITH BANKS

After you've succeeded in agreeing a Lease Option with a seller, the last thing you need is for the bank to stop it from progressing so you need to act in the right way.

The Financial Conduct Authority (FCA)

In the same way that only qualified people can give legal advice, only FCA regulated organisations or individuals can provide mortgage advice, so it is important that you don't tell people that they 'need not to worry about the mortgage.' Similarly, you should steer clear of advising the owner what to say

to his or her bank because that also counts as financial advice.

Debt plans

You will need to seek agreement to proceed on a Lease Option Debt Plan with the bank. The advantage of a debt plan is that it allows you to make guaranteed monthly payments direct to the lenders of the properties that you control. Never rely on the property owner to make payments to their mortgages. You must also have the confidence of knowing that your plan is set up correctly. Debt Management Companies deal with many high street lenders and banks on a daily basis. Leave it to the specialists to make sure everything is done correctly in setting up your Lease Option Debt Plan.

Heads of Terms

This is the one-page document you draw up with the seller setting out the terms of the Option. It is important to note that this is *not* legally binding. No

court will enforce a Heads of Terms if a seller decides to subsequently back out of doing a Lease Option. A seller who signs a Heads of Terms is not signing an Option Agreement. A Heads of Terms is simply a setting out of what a seller is going to agree to do. The advantage in drawing up a Heads of Terms is that it is useful for all parties to clearly see what they are agreeing to and it will go on to form the basis of the eventual Lease Option agreement drawn up by a qualified solicitor.

Consent to let

Consent to let is needed from the bank otherwise you will be in breach of insurance terms.

Purchase Option paperwork checklist

Heads of Terms (drawn up between you and the vendor)
Lease Option (drawn up by a solicitor)
The vendor signs the Lease Option & Power of Attorney

Sale Option (Tenant Buyer) paperwork checklist

Sale Option agreement (drawn up by a solicitor)
Residential Tenancy Agreement (the Tenant Buyer will sign this and this will be your protection. If the Tenant Buyer stops payments they will lose their upfront money and the Option will fall away).
Tenant Buyer's lawyer checks all the paperwork.

CHAPTER NINE

CASE STUDY – SEAN THOMSON

Thirty-six year old Sean Thomson is a successful property investor with numerous properties across the UK, and someone who has achieved his ambition of financial freedom. He came to the UK from South Africa in 2000 and got a job in Financial Analysis with *The Daily Mail,* but soon realised that this wasn't for him.

'I got fed up', he explains. 'I was working a forty hour week, which in practice turned out to be a sixty-five hour week and I felt something had to change.' That change occurred thanks to what Sean describes as his first 'sliding doors moment', referring to the

famous movie where the lead character's life suddenly changes onto a whole new path.

Sean says, 'I was standing in an airport bookstore, holding a copy of *Rich Dad Poor Dad*, the bestseller about personal finance by Robert Kiyosaki. 'If I hadn't bought that book I wouldn't be where I am today. It inspired me and showed me another way to become successful.'

Sean attended his first Tigrent Learning course in 2004 and at the end of that course came Sean's second 'sliding doors moment', when he decided to move forward and begin his new life in property investment.

Sean bought his first property in Burnley in 2004, for £26,000. He bought the property on credit cards and spent an additional £5,000 to improve it. The bank financed 80% of the improved value of £42,000, which basically meant he got paid to own a property.

'The results were amazing. The property was cash-

flowing at £150 a month. I had created 20% equity and pulled out all the funds in order to do the next deal. This set the trend for the future and became the formula I looked for in terms of return. Within 24 months I had achieved financial freedom.'

Subsequent to the property in Burnley, Sean went on to invest in properties across London but has now focussed his portfolio almost exclusively in South Wales. Sean uses a range of creative finance options to buy and hold, buy and sell and buy and develop, which includes turning commercial property into residential property.

Sean is enthusiastic about the power that Lease Options have for the property investor. He illustrates this with an example of one deal he did with a vendor who had refinanced his property and was desperate to move on. 'As the new mortgage was fixed, the vendor was faced with a 5% early repayment charge. The property was on the market to sell but at a higher price than the market value, so it wasn't attracting much interest.'

Sean was able to offer the vendor a solution to his problem. 'The vendor had thought about renting the property out but as he was moving thousands of miles away he didn't like the thought of managing a property from a distance. I suggested I take over the property on a fully repaired and insured lease and by doing this I was able to give him closer to what he needed price-wise. I also put a clause in the Option Agreement which prevented me from exercising the Option before the fixed rate mortgage period was up.'

Summarising the benefits to himself as the investor Sean says, 'I gained control of the property for a pound, I had no huge deposit to make and I didn't have to apply for a mortgage. I bought for £290K, refurbed for £60K and ended up with a property worth around £430K. Plus, I gained control for £6K rather than £75K.'

In addition to property investment, Sean is passionate about conservation, particularly in his native South Africa. The plight of the rhino, with the

scourge of poaching, and the importance of protecting natural resources is something he cares deeply about and he sees the financial freedom that successful property investment brings as a way of devoting himself to these concerns.

Sean's advice to someone looking to start a career in property investment? 'Firstly, never underestimate the importance of investing in yourself. The most valuable asset in a business is you. Knowledge gives you confidence and also allows you to take action in the right way.'

'I would advise people to get educated and learn about the different strategies that are available to you, like Lease Options. Not many people understand these things, so you can give yourself an advantage. The more skills and knowledge you have, the greater your ability to grow your business.'

CHAPTER TEN

CASE STUDIES

By now you will have an idea of how Lease Options work. Here are two scenarios that illustrate an example of a Purchase Option and a Sandwich Option. It is important to remember that the key feature of all Lease Options is their *flexibility*. There is no right way or wrong way to put together a Lease Option as long as it works for all parties and makes you a profit. These examples are intended to show the kind of imaginative ways you might construct a Lease Option as an investor.

Scenario One – Purchase Option

Ian and his three brothers inherited an unencumbered (no mortgage) property when their father passed away. It is a 3-bedroom detached house with a very large garden in a street full of semi-detached houses. The property has been on the market for three years. It was put on the market at £185,000 but it has slowly fallen to a current asking price of £150,000. The estate agent advises that this is still too high a value but the brothers are reluctant to reduce this any further. The brothers have been paying bills to keep the house heated but the boiler was stolen and the property now risks becoming derelict as it will not survive another winter without heat.

The following deal is an example of a Purchase Option.

You agree to a sale price of £130,000 based upon the condition of the property and its sale potential without a boiler.

Term: 2 years

Upfront consideration fee: £1

There are no monthly payments because there is no mortgage, except for a Council Tax of £1,200 per annum which you will pay.

There are no electric or gas bills because of the lack of boiler.

The refurbishment of the property will cost £15,000.

Once you have control of the property you apply for planning position to put another 3 bed house next door to create two semi-detached houses.

You can then put both semi-detached properties on the market for £135,000 each (the market value of a typical semi-detached house in the street).

Your research tells you that a 3-bedroom house can be built in this area for £60,000.

Profit Calculation:

Outgoings:

You are going to give the brothers £130,000 in 2 years.

Refurbishment costs: £15,000

Council Tax over 2 years: £2,400

Cost of New Build: £60,000

Total Outgoings = £207,400

Revenue:

Sale of two semi-detached houses at £135,000 each
= £270,000

Total Revenue = £270,000

Profit Potential after 2 years is:

£270,000 – £207,400 = **£62,600**

Scenario Two – Sandwich Option

John is an amateur landlord who is finding his 2-bedroom house difficult to manage. His experience with his lettings agent ended in disaster when his last tenant disappeared after trashing the property. The

estimated refurbishment costs for the house are £9K. The circumstances John finds himself in have made him a motivated seller and he has said that he is open to the idea of a Lease Option for a maximum of 5 years.

The following deal is an example of a Sandwich Option.

You agree to take over the property from John for £1.
You agree to pay John £300 per month to babysit the mortgage.
You agree a purchase price of £110,000.
Term: 5 years

To create a Sandwich Option you find a builder called James who agrees to buy the property from you for £1 and undertake all the refurbishment himself. He agrees to Rent To Buy at a sale price of £125,000 after 5 years. You also agree that he will pay you £600 per month in rent plus £208 per month as a top-up fee towards his deposit.

So, you are sitting in the middle of John the landlord and James the builder and this is how you make money on the deal:

Cashflow:

You are paying: £300 pcm to babysit John's mortgage.
You are charging James: £808 pcm (£600 rent + £208 top-up).
Therefore the cash-flow to you is: £508 pcm.
Over 5 years this works out as: £30,480 coming in.

Profit at the backend:

The purchase price was £110,000 and the sale price is £125,000 so the back-end profit is £15,000.

At the end of 5 years of paying £208 pcm top-up James the Tenant Buyer will have paid towards his deposit: £12,480. If James can secure a 90% loan to value mortgage he will need to pay a deposit of £12,500 so you can use the profit you have created

by selling the property to him at £125,000 to reimburse the £12,480 worth of top ups. This would leave us a residual profit of £2,520.

i.e. the total profit at the back end: £15,000 minus £12,480 = £2,520

This deal therefore has 3 potential profit centres:

1. The Option consideration fee: James the builder paid you £1 for the property and you gave that to John the landlord. So we didn't make any money at the front end.

2. During the Term of the Option Agreement, you took in £600 pcm and gave out £300 pcm, making you a profit of £300 pcm for 5 years which makes us £18,000 on the rent.

3. You have made £15,000 equity on the sale of the property (equivalent to the total rental top up payments and the residual profit).

And you will receive £2,520 when James completes the Option.

If we add together all the profit centres:

£18000 +
£12,480 +
£2,520

Total profit over 5 years = **£33,000**

CHAPTER ELEVEN

CONCLUSION

This introduction to Lease Options is designed to help the investor understand the potential benefits of this investment strategy. The key here is understanding how Lease Options, including Purchase Options and Sale Options (and Rent To Buy) work, how to find these opportunities, the advantages to the investor and the pitfalls to avoid. Knowledge is power and arming yourself with the right knowledge is crucial for success. A successful property investor should see Lease Options as a useful tool in their toolbox, giving them a flexible solution and a further way to make money from property. We wish you the very best of luck on your Brick Buy Brick journey.

This book is part of the Brick Buy Brick series, created in association with Tigrent Learning Ltd, who have been at the forefront of UK investment training since 2002.

www.brick-buy-brick.co.uk

NOTES

NOTES

NOTES

NOTES

NOTES

NOTES

NOTES